Land and Resources
OF ANCIENT EGYPT

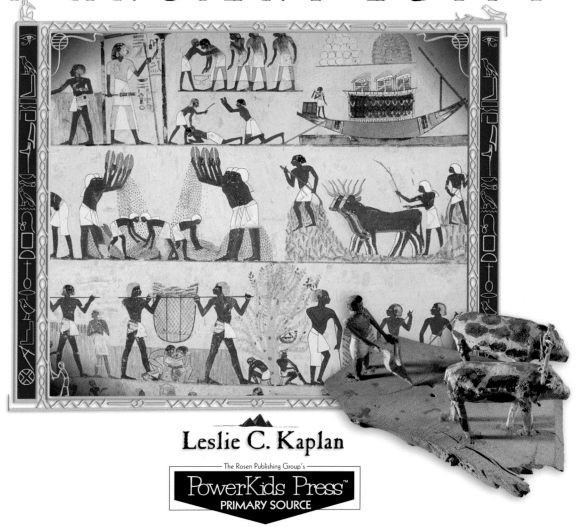

Leslie C. Kaplan

The Rosen Publishing Group's
PowerKids Press™
PRIMARY SOURCE

New York

To the Illmans

Published in 2004 by The Rosen Publishing Group, Inc.
29 East 21st Street, New York, NY 10010

First Edition

Editors: John Cassel and Joanne Randolph
Book Design: Maria E. Melendez
Photo Researcher: Adriana Skura

Photo Credits: Cover, title page, p. 7 (top right) © Kurt Scholz/SuperStock; cover, title page (inset), p. 8 © Gianni Dagli Orti/CORBIS; p. 4 © Michael Maslan Historic Photographs/CORBIS; p. 7 (top left) © NASA/GSFC/JPL, MISR Science Team; p. 7 (bottom) © Archivo Iconografico, S.A./CORBIS; pp. 12 (top), 15 (top), 16 (bottom) © The Granger Collection; pp. 11 (top), 12 (bottom), 20 The Art Archive/Dagli Orti; p. 11 (bottom) © SuperStock; pp. 15 (bottom), 16 (top) The Art Archive/Musée du Louvre Paris/Dagli Orti; p. 19 (top) The Art Archive/Egyptian Museum Cairo/Dagli Orti; p. 19 (bottom) © Scala/Art Resource, NY.

Kaplan, Leslie C.
Land and resources of ancient Egypt / Leslie C. Kaplan. — 1st ed.
    p. cm. — (Primary sources of ancient civilizations. Egypt)
Includes bibliographical references and index.
Contents: Geography of ancient Egypt—Black land and red land—The Nile River—A desert climate—People on the land —A land of plenty—Farming tools—Natural resources—Safe from attack—The gift of the Nile.
    ISBN 0-8239-6781-6 (library binding) — ISBN 0-8239-8931-3 (pbk.)
1. Egypt—Civilization—Juvenile literature. 2. Egypt—Geography—Juvenile literature. 3. Natural resources—Egypt—Juvenile literature. [1. Egypt—Civilization—To 332 B.C. 2. Egypt—Geography. 3. Natural resources—Egypt.] I. Title. II. Series.
    DT61.K346 2004
    333.7'0932—dc21   2002151558
Manufactured in the United States of America

Contents

An 1826 map of Egypt includes Lower Egypt in green, Upper Egypt in pink, and the Nile Delta, which was part of Lower Egypt, in yellow. Ancient Egyptians relied on the Nile River, which runs through the center of Egypt, to live.

Geography of Ancient Egypt

Ancient Egypt has been described by historians as a garden in a wilderness. A long, fertile strip of land was surrounded by a hot, dry desert. Between 3300 B.C. and 332 B.C., most early Egyptians settled along the ribbon of land that ran on either side of the Nile River. They also lived in the wide, triangular piece of land called the Delta in the north of Egypt, by the Mediterranean Sea. A delta is formed by the sediment left at the mouth of a river. Fierce deserts, in which the Egyptians could not live, lay beyond the banks of the Nile River. The Arabian Desert lay to the east, and the Libyan Desert lay to the west. Nubia was the land south of ancient Egypt.

The ancient Egyptians thought of their land as being divided into two main regions. They named each region for the color of its land. They called the Nile Valley *Kemet,* or "black land." Its soil was dark from the silt left after the Nile's flooding. Nearly all Egyptians lived in Kemet. It was the only place where crops would grow in Egypt. Desert surrounded this fertile land. The Egyptians called this land *Desheret,* or "red land." The name referred to the sand's reddish color and the heat of the sun. Desheret was too dry for growing crops. The Egyptians hunted animals and mined stone in the desert. They also buried their dead there. There was no room in Kemet for graves.

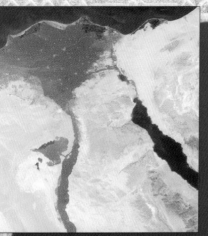

This present-day image of the northern day image of the northern part of Egypt shows the fertile green land along the Nile River and its delta. All the other land is hot, sandy desert. The Nile is the longest river in the world at about 4,160 miles (6,695 km).

These farming and fishing scenes from an ancient Egyptian tomb display the importance of the Nile and farming in daily life.

Nebamun, an Egyptian scribe, or writer, and grain counter of Thebes, hunts fowl on the Nile in this tomb painting from around 1425–1400 B.C.

Egyptians hunted for birds, such as geese and ducks, and found that the waters of the Nile were full of fish, such as tilapia. Tilapia were so plentiful that they stood for new life.

The Nile River

The people of ancient Egypt could not have lived without the Nile River. They depended on its waters for farming, fishing, and raising animals. Shipbuilding became a major business, or industry. People used ships for fishing on the Nile, and for traveling to nearby towns to trade goods. The Nile flooded its banks each year, leaving behind rich soil that fertilized the fields within the valley and delta areas. The flooding of the Nile was so important that the Egyptians created a calendar to keep track of when it would occur each year. The waters began to rise in June. The flood season lasted until November, when crops were planted. The harvest began in March.

A Desert Climate

The climate of Egypt has always been hot and dry. Except for the Nile Valley and the Delta, the land is completely desert. The Sun's steady heat and power astounded the ancient Egyptians. They worshiped the Sun as a god, Re, also called Ra, who helped all living things. Once the Sun set, there was a sharp drop in temperature. Chilly nights following hot days caused some ancient Egyptians to have colds and rheumatism. On a summer day, the temperature rose to about 100°F (38°C). On a winter day, it dropped to about 65°F (18°C). The few inches (cm) of rain that Egypt got each year fell in the north, on the Mediterranean coast.

Queen Nefertari, dressed in white, is surrounded by gods and goddesses in this tomb painting from 1279 to 1213 B.C. The Sun God Re is represented by the orange disk of the Sun.

Egyptians carved many statues to honor the Sun God, here called Amon Ra.

Ancient Egyptians had an advanced irrigation system that allowed them to bring the Nile's water to their farms.

Men used cattle to pull plows to prepare the land for planting. They planted such crops as dates, figs, olives, and grains. Date palms are shown at the bottom of this painting.

People on the Land

Ancient Egypt was one of the world's first civilizations. People began to settle along the Nile more than 5,000 years ago. In the deserts around the river valley, farming was impossible. The Egyptians needed the fertile land around the Nile to grow crops for food, clothing, and shelter. The Egyptians had to control the Nile's floodwaters to live through droughts and to water their fields. They learned to build dams and canals along the river. They used these irrigation systems to bring water from the Nile to their farms. These important building projects led to organization and teamwork among the people. Small towns grew into trading centers and areas of political and religious activity.

Farming became the main business of ancient Egypt. Egyptians grew flax, wheat, and barley in large amounts. They made cloth from flax. They made bread and beer from wheat and barley. The Egyptians grew onions, lettuce, and cucumbers, as well as melons, dates, and grapes. Animals, such as cows, sheep, goats, pigs, and geese, were raised for their skins, milk, or meat. In the swamps along the Nile, men hunted hippopotamuses and crocodiles for sport. People also ate and sold fish, such as carp and perch. Papyrus grew near the river. Before 2400 B.C., Egyptians invented paper made from this plant. It was used as a writing material for more than 3,000 years.

Grapes were one of the main crops grown in ancient Egypt. This painting from 1400 B.C. shows men picking grapes in a vineyard.

After harvesting the grains and making flour, Egyptians would make dough and bake it for bread.

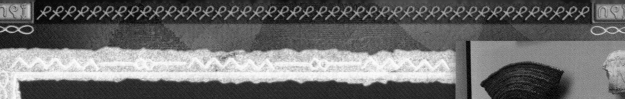

Egyptians created various tools, such as baskets and wooden hoes, to make farming easier.

This Egyptian man uses a shaduf to carry water that will be used for watering crops, cooking, or bathing.

The ancient Egyptians did much of their farming by hand, using simple tools. They used hoes and plows to break up the soil and to prepare it for seed planting. Sometimes cattle pulled the plows. The Egyptians used hoes to dig canals and carried baskets to collect the freshly dug mud. A tool called a *shaduf* made it easier to bring water from the canals to the fields. A shaduf consisted of a pole with a bucket at one end and a weight at the other. It helped the farmer to carry heavy buckets of water with less strain. The weight at the end of the pole balanced the bucket of water and spread the weight along the pole.

The Nile was ancient Egypt's most valuable natural resource. It provided fresh water and fish. People also used mud from the river's banks to build huts and to make pottery for cooking and storage. Egypt's deserts held natural resources as well. The ancient Egyptians dug for metals such as gold in their land's eastern and southeastern mountains. They used these precious metals to make jewelry, tools, and weapons. They mined stone from the desert, with which they made statues, temples, and tombs. Egypt lacked the wood needed for fuel and furniture. Egyptians traded for wood with merchants from neighboring lands, such as Nubia to the south and Syria to the northeast.

Gold and semiprecious stones were some of the resources that Egyptians were able to mine. They made decorations, such as the one shown above, out of these items or traded them.

This coffin, or sarcophagus, was created from stone and painted with dyes made from natural materials, such as plants or minerals.

People from neighboring areas are bringing gifts to Egypt's ruler, called the pharaoh, in 1504–1450 B.C. Some brought gifts in exchange for protection from Egypt. Others might have wanted to have a friendly relationship and to trade with Egypt.

Safe from Attack

The natural barriers of ancient Egypt prevented frequent attacks from outsiders. Extreme heat, lack of water, and wild animals, such as lions and cobras, made the Arabian and Libyan Deserts to the east and west of the Nile Valley unsafe to cross. Egypt also was protected from attack by the waterfalls and swamps of neighboring Nubia, to the south. The Red Sea to the east and the Mediterranean Sea to the north were other barriers. Sometimes enemies, such as the Hyksos, the Assyrians, and the Persians, interrupted Egyptian rule. Still, Egypt's ancient civilization lasted for nearly 3,000 years before being overthrown by Greek ruler Alexander the Great in 332 B.C.

The Gift of the Nile

The Nile River and its yearly inundation, or flooding, provided the basis for an important society. Without the Nile, Egypt would have been just desert. No fertile valley or delta in which people could settle would have existed. The river's floodwaters and the area's warm climate made plentiful harvests possible. Egypt grew to be one of the richest civilizations in the world. Natural barriers such as swamps and deserts helped to prevent enemy attacks, and civilization flourished along the Nile's banks. Egypt's people enjoyed many peaceful years, during which they developed a national government and created great works such as pyramids, sculptures, temples, and paintings.

Glossary

barriers (BAR-ee-erz) Things that block something else from
  passing.

droughts (DROWTS) Periods of dryness that cause harm to crops.

fertile (FER-tul) Good for making and growing things.

fertilized (FUR-til-yzd) Encouraged growth by adding something.

flax (FLAKS) A plant with blue flowers that is grown for its fiber.

inundation (ih-nun-DAY-shun) Flooding over.

irrigation (ih-rih-GAY-shun) To carry water to land through ditches or
  pipes.

papyrus (puh-PY-rus) A tall water plant, belonging to the sedge
  family, which was once plentiful in the Nile region of Egypt.

pottery (PAH-tuh-ree) Pots, vases, and similar objects that are made
  from clay.

pyramids (PEER-uh-midz) Huge structures that held the graves of
  Egyptian rulers, called pharaohs.

referred (rih-FURD) Made mention of; called attention to.

resource (REE-sors) A supply or source of energy or useful materials.

rheumatism (ROO-muh-tih-zem) A health condition causing pain in
  the muscles or joints.

silt (SILT) Fine bits of earth, smaller than sand grains, found at the
  bottom of lakes and rivers.

temperature (TEM-pruh-chur) How hot or cold something is.

tombs (TOOMZ) Graves.

Index

Primary Sources

Cover, title page. Havesting scene. Tomb painting. Menena Tomb, Valley of the Kings. Thebes, Egypt. **Inset.** Model of a farm worker plowing the fields. Clay model. Middle Kingdom, circa 2050–1786 B.C. Musée du Louvre. Paris, France. **Page 7. Top, right.** Tomb of the early Fifth Dynasty. Circa 2494–2345 B.C. Relief carved from stone. **Bottom.** Nebamun hunting fowl. Tomb painting. Circa 1425–1400 B.C. British Museum. **Page 8.** Hunting and fishing scene. Tomb painting. Circa 1400–1390 B.C. Chapel of Menna.Thebes, Egypt. **Page 11.** Fresco in the Tomb of Queen Nefertari, wife of Ramses II, surrounded by gods and goddesses. Circa 1200s B.C. Valley of the Queens. Thebes, Egypt. **Inset.** Statue of Amon Ra. Walters Art Gallery. Baltimore, Maryland. **Page 12. Top.** Nile River irrigation basin in an orchard. Tomb painting. Tomb of Sebekhotep. New Kingdom. **Bottom.** Sennedjem ploughing. Fresco. Tomb of Sennedjem, a servant in the Place of Truth. Circa 1320–1200 B.C. Deir El Medina, Thebes, Egypt. **Page 15. Top.** Egyptian vineyard. Tomb painting. Tomb of Nebamon. Circa 1400 B.C. Gourna, Egypt. **Bottom.** The making and baking of bread. Painted limestone. Circa 2500–2350 B.C. Musée du Louvre. Paris, France. **Page 16.** Egyptian man using a shaduf. Tomb of Ipouy. Circa 1275 B.C. Deir El Medina, Egypt. **Inset.** Wooden hoes and basket. New Empire. Musée du Louvre. Paris, France. **Page 19. Top.** Pectoral in gold and semi-precious stones with scarab. Treasure of Pharaoh Tutankhamen. Circa 1336–1227 B.C. Egyptian Museum, Cairo. **Bottom.** Sarcophagus of Thutmose IV. Tomb of Thutmose IV. Valley of the Kings, Thebes. **Page 20.** Foreigners bring tribute. Fresco. Tomb of Rekhmire, governor of Thebes and vizier to Thutmose III. Circa 1504–1450 B.C. Valley of the Nobles. Qurna, Thebes.

Web Sites

Due to the changing nature of Internet links, PowerKids Press has developed an online list of Web sites related to the subject of this book. This site is updated regularly. Please use this link to access the list:
www.powerkidslinks.com/psaciv/landegy/